Mel Bay's First Lessons® Violin

by Craig Duncan

CD CONTENTS

MEL BAY®

It doesn't get any easier.....

1 2 3 4 5 6 7 8 9 0

Visit us on the Web at www.melbay.com — E-mail us at email@melbay.com

Introduction

This text presents beginning violin technique and basic music reading fundamentals. There is an emphasis on using melodies and classical pieces to instruct each new concept. The 28 lessons include basic technique and reading skills, scales in the keys of A, D, G and C and bowing techniques such as dynamic contrast, slurs, accents, and staccato bowing. There are 47 melodies presented including works by Bach, Beethoven, Brahms, Handel, Mozart and other classical composers.

A CD recording of the book is available. It has all of the exercises and pieces recorded with solo violin and piano accompaniment. It is useful as a teaching and practice tool as well as a performance accompaniment track.

Contents

Lesson 1
Holding the Violin

Stand in an erect position with the feet shoulder width apart. Place the violin on the left shoulder, pointing outward to the side. Turn the head to the left and lower the left jaw and chin over the chin rest. The instrument should be supported entirely by the chin and shoulder, so that the left hand is free to note the instrument.

Practice holding the violin parallel to the floor using only the chin and shoulder for support. Place your left hand on your right shoulder and practice holding the violin with "no hands" for 30 seconds, then for a minute and then for two minutes. Do this several times daily until you are comfortable holding the violin with no support from your hands. The neck and shoulder muscles should be as relaxed as possible, using only enough tension to keep the violin from falling.

Many violinists find that a cloth or shoulder rest is helpful in supporting the instrument. There are many styles available. Experiment to determine what is best for you.

The index finger should touch the side of the violin neck at the knuckle adjoining the palm. The thumb should touch the opposite side of the neck above the thumb knuckle which is held in a straight position so that the end of the thumb is pointing upward. This placement will create an opening under the violin neck between the thumb, index finger and palm. The wrist is held with the palm away from the neck so that an imaginary line could be drawn from the elbow to the fingers. The left arm and elbow are held under the violin. The fingertips are to be placed on the strings with the knuckles bent.

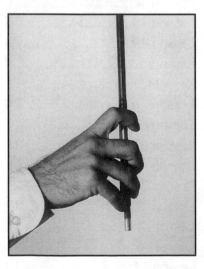
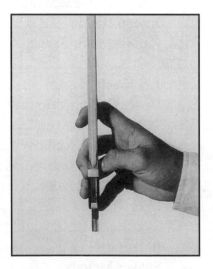
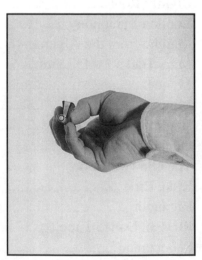

The first finger should touch the bow between the first and second joints. The middle and ring fingers should wrap around the bow comfortably, and the tip of the little finger should rest on the top edge of the bow. The fingers should be curved and spread apart. The end or tip of the thumb should be placed on the bow, forming a circle with the middle finger. The thumb knuckle is bent outward to eliminate tension in the right hand. The grip should be as relaxed as possible, using only enough tension to cradle the bow.

Practice finding the proper bow grip, releasing it, and finding it again at least twenty times before attempting to bow the violin. This is a good warmup exercise to use daily until the bow grip feels comfortable.

Photos by Charmaine Lanham

Playing the Open Strings

The names of the open strings from highest to lowest in pitch are E, A, D and G. They are notated on the following spaces of the treble clef.

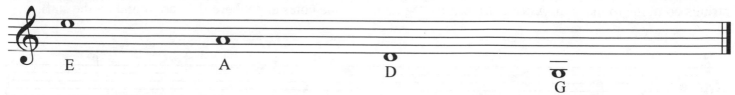

Place the bow on the E string midway between the bridge and the fingerboard. Pull the bow across the string in a downward motion toward the floor. This is called "down bow". The opposite direction is called "up bow". Practice going down and up bow several times on each string using short bow strokes. Try to keep the bow moving in a straight direction. It should stay at a ninety degree angle to the string. The right wrist should bend as the bow moves across the string. The right shoulder should be relaxed and the right elbow should stay level with the bow as you move from string to string.

Quarter Notes and Half Notes

The quarter note gets one beat and the half note gets two beats. The whole note gets four beats. The bow direction (down or up) is marked with the following symbols.

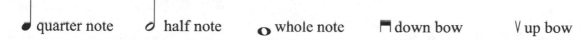

Practice these exercises, concentrating on straight bow strokes and clear tone.

 Track #2

Lesson 2

The notes in first position on the A string are open A, first finger B, second finger C# and third finger D. The notes on the E string are open E, first finger F#, second finger G# and third finger A. The notes on these two strings combine to make an A scale. Memorize the names of the notes and where they are found on the staff.

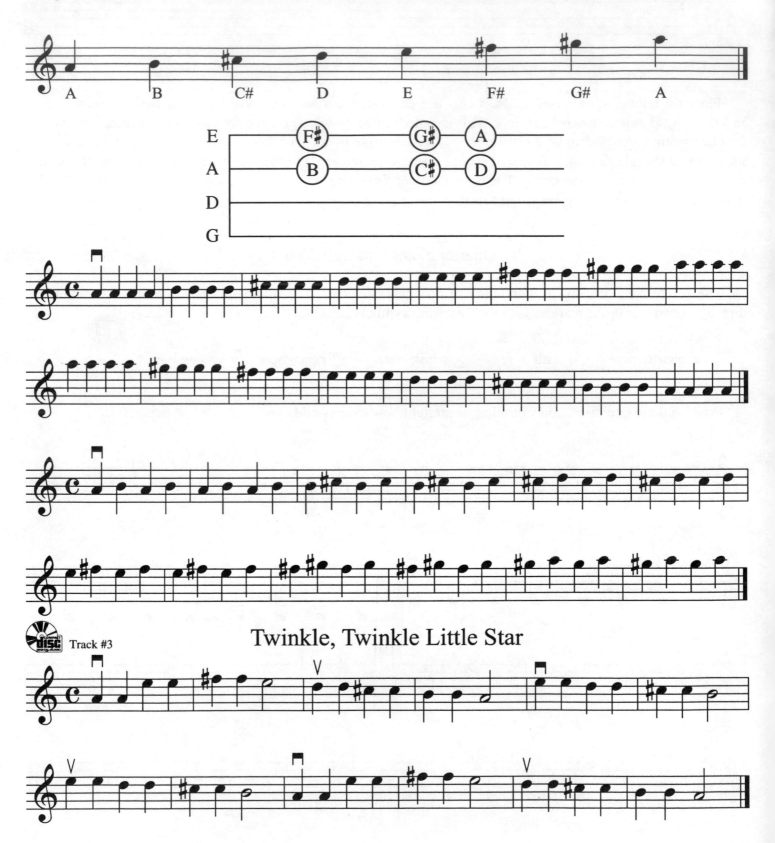

Track #3

Twinkle, Twinkle Little Star

6

Lesson 3

The flats or sharps used in the key of a piece of music are shown at the beginning of the staff. This is called a key signature. In the key of A, there are three sharps - F#, C# and G#.

Track #5

Mary Had a Little Lamb

Track #6

Jingle Bells

Lesson 4

At the end of *Russian Dance Tune* and *Lightly Row* there are two dots just before the final barline. This is called a **repeat sign** and indicates that the music is to be played again.

Russian Dance Tune

Lightly Row

Track #8

When a dot is added after a note, the length of the note is increased by half. Thus a two beat half note followed by a dot becomes a three beat dotted half note. Likewise, a one beat quarter note becomes a one and a half beat dotted quarter note.

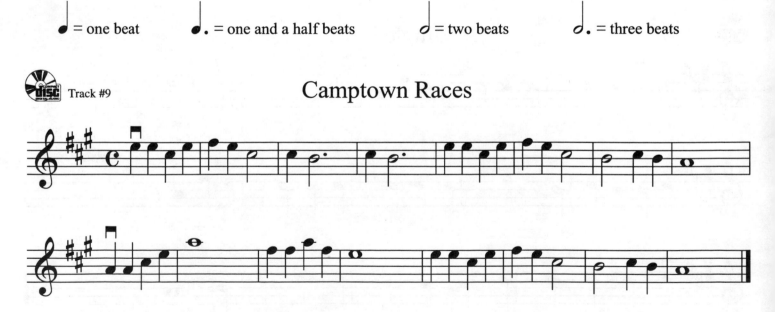

♩ = one beat   ♩. = one and a half beats   𝅗𝅥 = two beats   𝅗𝅥. = three beats

Track #9

Camptown Races

Lesson 5

The eighth note is equal to one half of a quarter note, so it usually gets one half of a beat. Eighth notes are counted by saying "1 and 2 and 3 and 4 and." When an eighth note follows a dotted quarter it comes on the "and" of the beat.

Track #11

Hungarian Folk Song Number 1

Bela Bartok

Track #12

The Old Gray Goose

Lesson 6

The notes in first position on the D string are open D, first finger E, second finger F# and third finger G. Memorize the names of the notes and where they are found on the staff.

Ode to Joy (Ninth Symphony Theme)

Ludwig van Beethoven

Rests

A rest is a symbol which means to be silent. There is a rest equal to the value of each kind of note.

Eighth rest ✷ = one half beat   Quarter rest ⸺ = one beat   Half rest ⬛ = two beats   Whole rest ⬛ = four beats

Scherzando

Bela Bartok

Lesson 7
D Scale

When two sharps, F# and C#, are found at the beginning of the staff, the music is in the key of D. A D scale can be played using the notes in first position on the D and A strings. Memorize the names of the notes and where they are played on your instrument.

Gavotte

Country Gardens

Track #16

Can, Can

Jacques Offenbach

Track #17

Lesson 8
Dynamics

The violin can be played louder or softer by changing three things:
1. The amount of bow pressure on the string; more pressure is louder, less pressure is softer.
2. The speed of the bow; faster bow is louder, slower bow is softer.
3. Closeness of the bow to the bridge; closer is louder, away from the bridge is softer.
The symbols for how loud or soft music is played are called **dynamic** markings.

ff double forte   *f* forte   *mf* mezzo forte   *mp* mezzo piano   *p* piano   *pp* double piano
very loud   loud   medium loud   medium soft   soft   very soft

Dixie

Largo from The New World Symphony

Anton Dvorak

Lesson 9

The notes in the key of D on the E string are open E, first finger F#, low second finger G and third finger A. The low second finger is placed on the string very close to the first finger creating a half step interval between the two fingers. The third finger stays in its same postion, leaving a whole step between second and third finger.

Track #21

Rigaudon

Henry Purcell

Lesson 10

At the beginning of the first staff just after the key signature is a symbol called the **time signature**. Everything found in the book so far has been in "common" time which is the same as 4/4. The tunes in this lesson are in 3/4. The top number in the time signature gives the number of beats per measure and the bottom number tells what kind of note is equal to one beat. In "common" time , marked with a C, and in 4/4 time there are four beats per measure and the quarter note is equal to one beat. In 3/4 time there are three beats per measure and the quarter note is equal to one beat.

Lavender's Blue

Allegretto

Ludwig van Beethoven

Lesson 11

A **slur** is a marking that connects two or more notes. All notes connected by a slur are played without changing the direction of the bow. A slur that connects two notes on the same pitch is called a **tie**.

Gavotte

Simple Gifts

Shaker Melody

Lesson 12
Accents

Accents are found on notes that are to be emphasized or played stronger than notes around them. This is done by applying more bow pressure at the beginning of the note. Once the note begins the pressure is lightened to the normal amount.

Fanfare Minuet

King William's March

Jeremiah Clarke

Lesson 13
Key of G

The key of G has only one sharp, F#. The second finger is placed low on the E string to play G natural and low on the A string to play C natural. The first finger pattern is used on th G string to play G, A, B and C. Memorize the names of the notes in the key of G and where they are on the instrument.

Track #29

London Symphony

Joseph Haydn

Lesson 14
Crescendo and Decrescendo

Crescendo means to play gradually louder and decrescendo means to play gradually softer. Sometimes the words or an abreviation (cresc and decresc) are used in the music. Other times the symbol < indicates crescendo, getting louder, and the symbol > indicates decrescendo, getting softer.

Jamaica

English Dance Tune

18

Lesson 15
The Upbeat

Music often begins with less than the full number of beats in the first measure. These notes are called pickups. The first beat of a full measure is called the downbeat and the last beat of a measure is called the upbeat. Upbeats are usually played up bow.

British Grenadiers

Symphony Theme

Johannes Brahms

Track #32

Lesson 16
Accidentals

Accidentals are sharps, flats or natural signs that are used when the note in the music is not in the key signature. They change the notes for only one measure at a time. In the following measure the notes in the key signature are used unless there is another accidental marking.

Minuet

Georg Philipp Telemann

Track #34

The Harmonious Blacksmith

Georg Frederic Handel

20

Lesson 17
Key of C

The key of C has no sharps or flats. The first finger pattern is used on the G string. The D string and A string have low second fingers. The first finger on the E string is also played low. This new finger pattern places the first finger an half step from the open string with a whole step between first and second and second and third fingers. Memorize the names of these notes and where they are played on the violin.

Track #36

Trumpet Minuet

Lesson 18

There are two lines to this tune. The top line is the melody or first violin part and the bottom line is the harmony or second violin part. Learn to play each part, then play a duet by putting the parts together with another musician.

The word **ritard** found at the end of the piece means to slow down.

French March

Lesson 19

Sometimes it is necessary to play two notes with the same bow direction but make them sound as if the bow direction changed. This is done by stopping the bow and then starting again, continuing the same direction. Try to make the notes sound as if each were a seperate bow stroke.

Track #39

Gavotte in C

Marche from the Algerian Suite

Camille Saint-Saens

Lesson 20

The fourth finger of the left hand is very important in playing the violin. In first position, fourth finger on the A string should sound the same pitch as open E, fourth finger on the D the same as open A, and fourth finger on the G the same as open D. Fourth finger on the E string is B.

Track #42

Bourrée from The Water Music

Georg Frederic Handel

Track #43

Etude

Nikolai Paganini

Lesson 21

There is often a choice of playing either the open string or the fourth finger. A good rule to follow is to use the fingering that makes the bowing smoother. For example, the first measure of this piece is played on the A string without a string crossing when the fourth finger is used to play the E.

Gavotte from Sonata No. 2, Opus 5

Georg Frederic Handel

Menuet

J. S. Bach

Lesson 22
Key of A

The key of A has three sharps, F#, C# and G#. A two octave scale can be played beginning with first finger A on the G string. The third finger on the G string is played a whole step higher than the second finger to note C#. The third finger on the D string is also played higher to note G#.

German Dance

Ludwig van Beethoven

Lesson 23
German Dance in A

Ludwig van Beethoven

Andante Grazioso

Wolfgang Amadeus Mozart

Track #48

Track #49

Lesson 24

Sixteenth notes have two flags and are half as long as eighth notes. In 4/4, 3/4 and 2/4 time there are four sixteenth notes in each beat.

Ride, Ride

Dmitri Kabalevsky

Bonaparte's Retreat

Track #51

Theme used by Aaron Copland for Rodeo

Lesson 25

The dotted eighth gets three fourths of a beat. It is equal to the length of three sixteenth notes. Make certain to make it last three times longer than the sixteenth note in these melodies.

Soldier's March

Robert Schumann

Theme from the Fourth Symphony

Franz Schubert

Lesson 26

Staccato markings are dots found over or under the note head. They indicate that the note is to be played with a shorter bow stroke, stopping the bow before the full value of the note sounds. This leaves space between the notes giving them a "short" sound.

Glockenspiel

Wolfgang A. Mozart

Lesson 27

The following tunes have staccato notes and full length notes. Be certain to make a difference in the style by leaving space between the staccato notes while the bow is stopped and playing full bow strokes on the notes that are not staccato.

Surprise Symphony

Joseph Haydn

Gavotte in D

Arcangelo Corelli

Lesson 28

Grace notes are small notes written just before a regular size note. They do not last the normal length, but are played quickly. In some pieces they are played on the beat and in other pieces they are played before the beat.

Sonatina

Ludwig van Beethoven